THE
LANGUAGE
SOLUTION

THE LANGUAGE SOLUTION

HENRY WALOSIK

Copyright © 2023 Henry Walosik.

All rights reserved. No part of this book may be reproduced, stored, or transmitted by any means—whether auditory, graphic, mechanical, or electronic—without written permission of both publisher and author, except in the case of brief excerpts used in critical articles and reviews. Unauthorized reproduction of any part of this work is illegal and is punishable by law.

ISBN: 979-8-88640-764-8 (sc)
ISBN: 979-8-88640-765-5 (hc)
ISBN: 979-8-88640-766-2 (e)

Because of the dynamic nature of the Internet, any web addresses or links contained in this book may have changed since publication and may no longer be valid. The views expressed in this work are solely those of the author and do not necessarily reflect the views of the publisher, and the publisher hereby disclaims any responsibility for them.

One Galleria Blvd., Suite 1900, Metairie, LA 70001
1-888-421-2397

CONTENTS

Prologue 1

The Problem 3

The Pros and Cons 5

Steps to be Taken 8

Let's Do It 18

Conclusion 36

Epilogue 39

PROLOGUE

The author of this book is a German born son of Polish immigrants who chose to emigrate to Canada, to seek a better life for themselves and their children, after the second world war when they became refugees in Germany. He grew up in the North-western region of Quebec (Val-d'Or) where he spoke only the Polish language until the age of five.

At the age of five years old, he was integrated into English school and apparently was very scared on his first day in school not being able to communicate in any other language but Polish. The second day of school was already better and he was on his way to learning English. The French language was also taught in school and progressively became fluent in French also.

When he married into a French speaking family he and his Wife were determined to raise the children they would have in both English and French. The couple have three boys who are fluently bilingual and the same for their six grand children. This is not the end because the grand children will carry this on without any difficulty and from one generation to another the number of bilingual people will grow.

The author wrote this book to show the general public that to become a bilingual person is not such a big thing. If the public at large can muster up enough support for such an endeavour, all Canadians will be beneficiaries of stability and peace of mind. He is of the opinion that this is the best route to take to kill the idea of Separation which, if attained, guarantees absolutely nothing concrete. He believes that Canada has not yet reached the heights that for it is possible and a strong harmonious atmosphere could propel it to the most envious country in this modern world.

We must not forget that human nature is inclined to help one another and here is a challenge that Canadians should grasp to show mankind their resolve. There will not be only one winner but millions of them when in time the country becomes more and more bilingual. One would think that a politician some where would have thought up such a scheme but language sometimes is a touchy subject. Although it may be a hard sell at the beginning, the politicians have to put their personal agendas aside and direct their energy towards making this a dream come true.

Go Canada go!!!!!!!!!!

THE PROBLEM

Is the French-English question that big of a problem? This has been going on for hundreds of years and nobody in the political circle seems to have an answer. Everybody involved in this matter seem to twist and turn their observations so as to profit from their conclusions.

Day after day, month after month and year after year, the antagonists accuse each other of betrayal and lack of understanding. The ordinary Joe Blow on the street, not interested in the haggling going on, takes a position on the subject according to his convictions and often not to the betterment of all. The problem only gets worse and becomes a painful burden for those who would like it to be solved.

This language thing has been draining public funds, that could have been used to advance the country and has, instead, sunk it into perpetual antagonism. It is high time for all the common folk to stop and think where the politicians are leading us to with this unsolved puzzle. We mustn't forget that it will be us, the public that will pay for the consequences of decisions taken for egoistic purposes. The politicians always have a way out of these embarrassing situations by blaming it on their opponents or by disappearing from the public view. In Quebec and Canada, we have been supporting political parties whose goal is to break up the country and yet after over thirty years of attempting to do so have failed to enhance the cause. The continuation of allowing this situation to thrive will create a fault within Canadian society and all the different regions of Canada will slowly pull away from the core of the country and will seek political freedom. In such a case, the nation will probably divide into four parts i.e . . . . Quebec, Ontario, Eastern and Western Canada.

THE PROS AND CONS

Canada is blessed with an abundance of natural resources and this in its entirety, so, economically, each fraction that would separate from the whole could survive without the aid of the other parts. Gold, silver, lithium and titanium are only some of the riches present in Canada's earth formations. These are God given gifts that we should develop together as a united country and not taken over by foreign interests because we are divided. The country's crust is rich in minerals of all types and origins such that with the advancement of present day technology, discovery and extraction methods are well on their way to cost efficiency thus producing handsome returns on investment. We have to examine our conservative ways and put more of our savings into the country's capital needs for new prosperous developments. Taking this route will establish us as "Maitre" at home and we would reap the wealth and not foreigners.

Canada also has the forest to turn to for wealth, however; this commodity is cyclical and has caused a lot of hardships the last few years because of the economic crisis in the U.S.A. Once again, the nation should be looking for ways to improve the stability of this sector by using creativity to find new products that would help it prosper continuously without having disastrous lows as is the present scenario. Steps have to be taken so we can reduce considerably our dependence of selling our forest products to the States. The U.S., when its dollar out values ours, takes advantage and buys limber at rock bottom prices thus preserving their own forests. Our forest industry is very important to us and we should be going out of our way to make sure it always remains in a healthy stage. Many livelihoods are affected by the degree of success this part of the economy is having. Generation after generation have laboured in our forests as to be able to put food on the table on a daily basis. The jobs they hold when the sector is well and running, provide them with decent salaries which permit them to live comfortably.

Finally, Canada is rich in oil with the tar sand in the west and Hibernia in the east. Other discoveries are being made such as the deposit off the Magdalene Islands which by itself contains a huge quantity of oil to make us self sufficient. We also could supply our neighbour to the south without affecting our own needs. Routes have already been proposed to get the western oil to customers in the U.S. and Asia. The U.S. route has been stalled due to the possibility of a major spill on barren forests. A decision has been postponed until after the American elections thus eliminating this subject as an argument for one or both American political parties. The route to send the oil to Asia is under study and is being scrutinized for possible disasters from a spill. So, we know we have lots of oil and countries like China and India who are in the midst of rapid expansion have already made it clear that they would become consumers of this petroleum.

All these natural resources are ours for the taking, however; we must go at it as a united Canada with friendly ties between the provinces and a harmonious relationship with the central government in Ottawa. The only way we will grow and prosper is by rolling up our sleeves and forming one big family across this land and advancing our knowledge with vigour and determination to develop new markets. Every thing is there, in place, for us to achieve this great Moment. We have to bury the war hatchet before it destroys everything we believe in and have worked to attain. We can't let the path of "separation" fall between us and a rich tremendous future that is there for the taking. Let us become open minded like the Europeans who settled here in Quebec and became trilingual. None of these people really gave up their origins as Pole, Ukrainians or Germans but still learned the French and English dialogues.

STEPS TO BE TAKEN

Although Canada has everything going for it, enabling it to be a world leader in all aspects, there is one issue that never fades away and continues to be a thorn in its side and that is the language difference. The two founding languages (after the first nations) have not been able to reach a common ground of respect. Ever since French and English explorers set foot on this land called Canada, the two peoples have always disputed land claims and sovereignty and this abnormal behaviour has prevented them from forming a strong and long lasting federation.

When the English defeated the French on the Plains of Abraham, it was thought that maybe, finally, this matter would have an ending but to no avail, the French had the resolve to get back up and fight for their rights. They started by demanding the protection of their mother tongue in the Province of Quebec which was seemingly being assimilated by the English language. There started to be proof of this concept as more and more French children were switching to English school. This movement did not give the Quebec government of the day any choice and Law 101 came to life. The only thing wrong with this undertaking is that it prohibited the freedom of French parents from sending their offspring to English schools whereas English parents had the right to choose. The passing of this law might have saved the French language from diminishing, however, it prevented French children to learn English which is a necessary tool for anyone who wants to be successful in North America and as well as the whole planet as English is the business dialect everywhere.

Furthermore, the adoption of Law 101 most likely had a negative effect on the minority of the French populations in the other Provinces. The aspect of free trade made it easier for people to leave any given Province for another one but the unfortunate Quebecers who do not have any English requires most of them to remain in Quebec because speaking both languages is a pre-requisite for hiring. We have to take some gigantic steps to deal with these discrepancies because they cause tensions between the two different cultures that are very important for the Country to achieve its fullest possibilities. It seems as if it is always the French that end up with the short part of the rope. We must always remember this when Quebec is negotiating a language dispute with the federal government but of course we can not always accord them what they want.

In the far past, Quebec, being a predominant Catholic society, was almost forced to have children every year by the Church who was insuring its domination of the masses. Eventually, the practise was ended when a more educated French population realized what the Church was up to. Today, people still admit to adhere to the Roman Catholic faith, but very few practise it causing the closure of many churches across the province. Then, there is the lack of priests who are becoming scarce because there are not even enough replacements in the seminaries. The future does not look promising for the Church and maybe we need some drastic changes from the Vatican. The Vatican must upgrade the standards of the Church in accordance with today's mentality which differs extremely with the old teachings.

Canada no longer can afford not to face the music and definitely has to redirect its language differences before a third party comes up the middle and creates a majority. Does anybody realize that the main spoken tongue in Toronto is no longer English and as a matter of fact not French either? The two official languages here are in a minority and who is willing to take the blame? The solution, excluding the politicians, should be made by the Canadian people as a whole. Every citizen has to put his pants on and take his responsibility of seeing the fact that all Canadians are treated equally in both official languages and this from coast to coast. There are, at the Moment, too many minorities that are entering this country and using their native tongues without learning one of the main languages. Doing this causes segregation and many communities become populated with certain nationalities that use their own language more frequently.

Up to the present time, the majority, though it is slim, loath the idea of the country breaking up. We should not let the balance swing so we have to do something now and not when it is too late. We saw an example of that in the 1995 Referendum when drastic steps, not all quite legal, were taken to save the country. The only way we will bury the separatists is if we offer the French faction equal rights and these rights must be available throughout the country. Reciprocally, Quebec must be willing to do the same in the Province of Quebec. All we have to do is examine countries in Europe and Latin America where students learn up to three dialogues or, in some cases, more. A great number of Canadians take great measures to speak in Spanish when they go south in the winter. Why can't we give the same importunity to learning the two official languages in our own country? Something does not add up here, both main cultures in this country are guilty of the gap that exists between them.

The solution to our inner problem is that both English and French be considered compulsory subjects in school thus making the country bilingual. If anyone would look around and account for all the young Europeans that immigrated to Canada, we would be surprised to know what percentage is bilingual. Kids, who are very young, will learn both English and French and quite easily. Many Europeans that came to Quebec after the war have children, grandchildren and even great grandchildren that read, write and speak both languages making them true Canadians. They are not obliged to side for one or the other being able to converse in both languages, what an advantage.

Many French parents express their will to have their children speak English because of the English omnipresence that surrounds Quebec but are prevented from doing so because of adverse political decisions. However, these politicians do not hesitate to send their offspring to educational facilities elsewhere in Canada where they apprehend the English language. They definitely do not follow the popular proverb that states "what is good for the goose is good for the gander". The Quebec people must take a firm stand and oblige the governments at all levels that they desire to have their children fluently bilingual by the end of high School and this should also apply to the English population in the opposite way. At this Moment, there are French citizens in Montreal who are deprived of services in the French language which is a sacrilege in the context that Montreal is in a predominantly French Province and everyone should be able to find any kind of service in French. Let us not make the same mistake again and run the chance of losing our English rights in a separate Quebec.

Protection of the French faction by law should not antagonize one group against the other but encourage both groups to work with each other to strengthen our Canadian identity. If the vast majority of Canadians and Quebecers were bilingual, could you imagine the harmony that would be omnipresent. Hell, John Lennon's legacy would be proven here in Canada and maybe influence major changes for our close neighbours to the South. The proof is there that most of the immigrants to our native land learn, at least, one of the two official languages and many more than we think learn both of them.

It is not an impossible dream to believe that our nation can become a fantastic example to the rest of the world by taking the required measures to install bilingualism across this country and then this attribute would spread from generation to generation without any drawbacks. All we need is the good will of one and all to make it a personal challenge to contribute to the unity of this great land of ours. We once had the title of "Great Peacekeepers", so, why can't we regain this prestige by doing what has to be done to live in peaceful harmony in our own entourage. The result of our adherence to such a well planed conversion could not be anything but an enormous benefit to the citizens of Canada.

The voters of this country should, time is of the essence, oblige by way of referendum or public meetings, our political parties to establish this endeavour in their political platforms and make it an electoral promise in order to be chosen to govern the nation or province. Education being a provincial jurisdiction should not be an excuse for its non-implantation. The final method to achieve the goal has to be a well documented project that will be accepted by everybody from one corner of this land to the other. When people brainstorm, there can only be positive suggestions put on the table if they are convinced that what will be done can only enhance the reputation of the country.

We must act now, without hesitation, if we do not want the question of separation to creep up on us again and maybe even be successful. A person whose roots are in, let's say, Poland will never be anything else but Polish in his heart, however, this does not prevent him from being a loyal Quebecer and a full fledged Canadian. Creating a bilingual Canada is the only way every citizen can be a part and a whole at the same time. If someone says that this is a unattainable solution, it is because he or she do not believe in equality for everyone.

English Canada should be the player to introduce this measure in order to display its intention to make such an undertaking succeed. If all the provinces and territories, outside Quebec, agreed on this perception, it is quite likely that French Canadians would join this attainable proposition. Starting from the first grade in school, both languages would be taught by capable experienced teachers and before we would know it, we would be on our way in creating a new and understanding society. It is when we are young that learning languages is the easiest. Thus, teaching them when children start school would not really create a burden and in a few years these students would be able to live in both languages and pass this on to their children and so on. The mother tongue could be (as Europeans did) used at home, satisfying everyone. Jobs would be much easier to obtain and the employers would have better access to all the markets in the country. Let us not be fooled, a step in this direction will not be an easy chore to get up and running unless the whole country realizes that it is high time to bury the hatchet and get on to building this Country into a great and prosperous nation.

We, already, are one of the most advanced performers in the mining and forestry industries of the world. Many countries look up to us when it comes to implanting mines and saw mills thus acknowledging our expertise in these fields. Hundreds of our mining employees are being employed in places like Africa and Latin America. Experience is what they are all seeking and know that Canada has an abundance of such personnel. Soon, with metal prices sky rocketing due to the fast growing economies in China and India, the world will see shortages of manpower in the mining sector. This lack of qualified people will give those who are bilingual an advantage to nail down the best paying jobs.

In the Abitibi region of Quebec, it is believed that there will be openings for miners in the thousands so Companies will have to seek workers in other countries which will lead to an immigration boom one more time. The Province of Quebec will have to be careful so that these newcomers' intentions will be to adopt the French tongue when they arrive. The occasion to start a whole new system of schooling to encourage these groups to become bilingual is essential and would enable us to demonstrate to the rest of Canada that we are willing to participate in a unified Canada but our predominance of the French language in the Province must be defended at all costs.

The other Provinces and Territories will also benefit from the many mining projects that will be put into production in the near future, in their regions. All these economic moves will have for an effect the movement of workers from every point in Canada to another. If the language situation didn't cause any downfalls, wouldn't it be a success story? Remember, language does not a man or woman make, it only is a tool to communicate one's ideas to another. It is a preservation of a culture that doesn't have to be in danger of assimilation just because another language is spoken. We have to stop using this as a reason to implement strict language laws. The solution is at the tip of our fingers, waiting to be put forth and agreed upon by all.

Sports is another domain where players from many different nationalities form a team and try, with team work, to win the representative cup or coveted trophy. Once again it is the European players that lead the way and learn, be it English or French because they need one or the other to be able to express themselves. Does that mean they are separating from their roots? Bull, they have the common sense to admit that it is to their advantage to study the dialogue they will need to put their ideas in perspective. The people who think that you can change a French person in Quebec and make his identity change into some other language has a lot to learn about the French Canadian culture. French Canadians possess a "Joie de Vivre" that does not exist anywhere else in Canada and they have no problem in showing this in the way they live. Sporting events are a way for Canadians to socialize but Quebecers are very much more demanding than their counterparts and hate to lose. The strain, especially in hockey, is sometimes overwhelming and very hard to endure mentally. Hockey is the sport that several French Canadians choose as a career and excel in. Even here, the language context is a matter of verbal altercations. In certain circumstances when the games become physical, French players are victims of language slurs which are abhorrent isolated, unnecessary happenings. The funny part, it is to a great extent the English participants that are guilty of these distasteful acts. Again, if all or most of those involved in this sport were bilingual, the tendency to choose such intimidation would cease. Hell, we are all Canadians, so let us all live and work in harmony and respect for each other's language and culture. Any other way is a sign of great ignorance and hatred.

One sport predominantly practised in the English parts of Canada that has become and is increasing in popularity in French Canada is University football. Since a few years, the French University teams are winning their share of National Titles creating competition that can only be healthy for the well being of our Country. Even better, French athletes are piercing the ranks of professional football teams both in Canada and the U.S.A. which was nowhere to be seen only a few years ago. This only proves, quite openly, where there is a will, there is a way. We should apply this proverb to our language situation and then reap all the positive ness this step would produce.

Many Canadian students, both English and French, are being offered scholarships in American schools due to their sport capabilities which is something we can make grow if we were a bilingual country. Young students, eligible for these scholarships, would not be held back because they didn't understand English. Likewise, students from across Canada and the world for that matter, could come to Quebec and study an advanced French.

Wow!!!!!! This is starting to be exciting. Be assured that if we put our efforts into it, we could succeed in being one big family from coast to coast and develop this country as no other country has done. We have to build trust and confidence amongst ourselves and help each other in obtaining self sufficiency in almost everything we need. Real wealth would result and would enable us to insure that all our citizens receive their due. Nothing works better then team work and we must strive to make it happen now and not let any language diversity come around and try to destroy it again.

Politicians choose to advance choices that only serve to give them greater power in enhancing their party's platform and do not care how this affects the ordinary citizen who is seeking a better life where he could pay fair taxes for the emancipation of this nation and not for ideas that are regularly throw out the window. We must, once and for all, push, the people who govern, into establishing laws that concern the betterment of our society and not serve the elevation of their political objectives. We must not forget the fact that it will be us and nobody else who will encase the results of decisions taken by these representatives who are elected to improve the quality of life of all citizens but who fail to do so. There is absolutely, a tremendous need, for the public to become a part of decisions taken which affect the core structure of this country of ours. The input of the people can only help harmonize our wish to be treated equally across the land and especially in our choice of the two founding dialogues. We, definitely, should not settle for less.

Quebec and Canadian film making has come a long way and the movies produced are getting excellent revues by moviegoers. Montreal has a firm that is quite outstanding in the production of special effects and its services are frequently sought by American film makers. No one would ever have dreamed of such an exploit just a ways back. French films attract a lot more Quebecers and their Translations a lot more English Canadians then ever before. All we need now is for Canadians and Quebecers to form partnerships and pool their resources to become as good as the Americans. This is not an impossible dream, it can be done easier than we think. Let's join hands, put our heads together and show the world what we are capable of. We can sell both our cultures in this way without having to downgrade one or the other.

LET'S DO IT

We have to get this language problem out of our way as soon as possible and the sooner we take steps to get it done the better. Our children and grandchildren will be the beneficiaries once it becomes a reality. All the provinces and territories of Canada should take the initiative and push their governments to set up a full proof French education program beginning from the first grade and going right up to the end of high school. The French, in the Province of Quebec will realize that the rest of the country is serious and in turn will set up a similar project to teach the kids English in Quebec. This would not be a huge burden to implement, however, the benefits that would result are not measurable. The rights of the French minority would have to be protected in the Province of Quebec and the working dialogue would be French. In the other parts of Canada, the English language would predominate except when warranted. An example of this would be Hearst, Ontario, where more than three quarters of the citizens are French. This town has not lost its French Heritage and the dialect spoken here is overwhelmingly French. The reason why Hearst has remained French is simply that it wanted to remain French and not be assimilated by the English.

English Canada has the responsibility to show its French minority that it is important to keep its identity as a culture existing within another one. If such an intervention occurs FRENCH Canada will hop on board and only then will we be able to say good bye to separation. There is room for everybody in this great and vast country, we just have to iron out the differences and following this, the entire population of Canada will get the opportunity to emancipate. We need not be hostages to Quebec as we have been in latter years to show them we insist they stay as part of this country. If we demonstrate our willingness to participate in a bilingual language project, the Province will surely accept such an undertaking. Think of it, European countries and others offer different dialogues in their schools and the children learn as much as three languages besides theirs. Canadians are just as bright as any other nation and is made up of various ethnic groups thus making it multicultural.

After the second world war, there were many Europeans that immigrated to the North-western region of the Province of Quebec to work in the gold mines that were flourishing but were having problems recruiting manpower. The flood of these newcomers turned that neck of the country into a multilingual society. French was not the working language and the English hierarchy steered the children of these strangers to the region to English schools. The French people never realized, even up to this day, that the immigrants were not given the chance to choose the tongue of education for their young ones. No big deal, the great majority of these kids ended up learning French and even remained in the region when the working language switched from English to French. Furthermore, the next generation also learned both languages proving that the more languages you knew, the better for you.

A myth grew out of the fact that the immigrants were sending their children to English schools to spite the French and force them to speak English. What a contortion of the truth, people who decided to keep on living here are not at all against the French language being the more popular of the two or else they would have packed up and left like many hard core English people did, despising the French. Today, a great number of French people still think ethnic groups vote against them in favour of English convictions. The ones that do are really mistaken because we vote on proven facts and not on dreams that may be unrealistic.

We, Québecers, should definitely give the rest of Canada an occasion to show its good will concerning this matter If we are serious in our convictions to settle this dispute for good, we have to be flexible both ways and constitute a win-win agreement that will allow this country to grow and prosper acceding to its capabilities. If we impute a peaceful atmosphere across this great land of ours, imagine the new heights we could attain by collaborating with each other to concretize different objectives. This in turn would create jobs and wealth for everyone, something we thrive for. Instead of continuing to bicker over our differences let us make it known to our politicians that we will not settle for anything less then a permanent solution which will propel Canada into bilingualism. Only when this is a forgone happening, will everyone in this country take his rightful place in a federation treating all its citizens with respect and equality. We mustn't, at all costs, allow the political arena to keep using this issue to arrive at their means. If we line up together and force the levels of government that have authority over this subject, we will come out winners for having done so.

There needs to be unanimous agreement for such an endeavour to become reality. However, if English Canada should not wish to cooperate, the only outcome should be the separation of Quebec. We can not keep pouring money in to this field and not come up with an answer any longer. Canadians are starting to get fed up with this subject that always seems to come back and haunt us. We either form one big family and sit at the same table or else we split up and go each our way.

Quebecers have a legitimate concern of being assimilated because in the past they have been pushed into speaking English to be served in public places in a Province populated by people of French descent. In a modern democracy such an obstacle seems rather ridiculous and a non sense. The French culture is a way ahead of the English one in terms of openness and the love of life. One just has to look at what happens on bordering cities to realize that the "train de vie" is much more explosive on the French side. Nobody seems to complain about this phenomena because it is acceptable by everyone. French woman, no offence intended, dress up much better than their English counterparts, something that is no big secret. In no way are French people more superior than the English, however, their living manners definitely outdo the other.

If Canada became bilingual, at the Moment it is a multicultural society, people would mix much more socially and probably instigate a true new Canadian culture to which all could adhere.

This great step would lead to national unity and inner pride towards being a French or English Canadian. Ethnic groups could preserve their original cultures at home and still be part of this updated modern Canadian entity. In this respect, the two founding nations policy would become the main dialect from coast to coast but it would be enhanced by traditions that other peoples would bring from somewhere else.

We can not prevent this country from continuing to be multicultural due to the need we have to increase the manpower in regions where we are extracting natural resources which are in great demand in countries who are experiencing tremendous expansions such as China and India. Never the less, the augmentation of our population in these places only presents us with the reality that many of these new citizens will not speak either French or English. So, why not start right now by putting in place in our schools, a language program that would meet all the requirements laid down by an agreement between the Provinces and Territories. There is no reason why any part of Canada would refuse such a proposal because it would be a fantastic step forward towards the unification of this great country, Canada. Minority groups from the entire planet will form a majority, if this is not already the case, and by imposing a language program on these immigrants, we will be able to secure the two founding tongues without any hassles. The new arrivals need not give up their perspective heritages which they could continue recognizing amongst themselves but would have to make an honest attempt to learn both French and English.

The language program would be one of the criteria to be accepted to come to this country as an immigrant. People who emigrate to other countries have no choice but to learn the language of the land. They are not given the choice of the dialect they must use. Therefore, although we believe deeply in being a democratic society, we have to see to it that those who want to live here must learn the two languages that are considered acceptable.

There it is in a nutshell, let us come up with something honest, concrete and acceptable to the people already making up this truly free country of Canada and to those who would like to become part of it. We can make this a nation of nations populated by humans who are open minded when it comes to language disputes and adopt a plan for the future that will appeal to everyone without any exceptions. Living here, in any part, would be advantageous, economically and socially because of the peaceful harmony that would reign. The dream of a great number of Canadians would finally become a reality which was once thought to be impossible. Everything is attainable if a strong will to implement radical changes for the benefit of all is present. We mustn't let those who want to break up this country to gain headway and destroy everything we believe in. Those who have taken the stand that the French and English are non-reconcilable are simply prophets of doom and gloom who would like to impose their personal outlooks on the population.

In these modern times, people are educated to a much higher degree than before and have come to the conclusion that politicians do not necessarily believe in the party's policies but adopt them just to get elected. It must come to the point that the people will have to set forth policies that will result in the acceptance of laws which will apply to the principal choices advanced by the majority of the voters. The political platforms must represent the will of the people or else there is no use in having elections. Today, the percentage of the population that exercises its right to vote unveils what people think of their politicians, a big farce. The different parties are said to be of the same nature that is to get their point across without, most of the time, carrying out the promises they made during the election period.

If we want this country to grow and prosper, we have to, as a collectivety, organize ourselves to inform our politicians that we will decide what is best for us as a society and that we will no longer endure the wasting of our tax dollars on frivolous matters concerning party policies. When this becomes a reality, people will once again vote in greater numbers because the issues will touch us all. It is high time, that Canada becomes the people's country and that the persons who are elected to represent the people do so with integrity and honesty. This comportment, in turn, will raise Canada to a great height where it truly belongs.

As of today, there is no threat of Canada being broken up but we all know that things change very fast in this new global picture that has become very transparent with the arrival of social media. People are emigrating to other countries to earn their livings and Canada is no exception. If we do not become strong, language wise and other, we will wake up one morning and realize that we are no longer 'Maitre Chez Soi". New immigrants are arriving in Canada, year after year, demanding to be able to keep their cultures and traditions which is putting a strain on the Canadian people. This is why we have to introduce laws so that the children of these newcomers learn both founding languages thus protecting our bilingual stature. In this context, Canada can only benefit and will continue being strong and prosperous.

All people have heard the expression "The American Dream", now, Canadians could create "The Canadian Dream» by showing their resolve to unite this country once and for all and guarantee its future. The "Canadian Dream" is attainable if everyone believes in freedom and equality. This would be the death of language referendums and the birth of a long lasting co-existence between the English and French population of Canada.

In the future Canada, jobs would be easily accessible to everyone, services of all kinds would be available in one or both of the official languages and the broad outlook for advancing the country forward, economically and socialy, would be tremendous. So, yes, now is the time to take that step forward and propulse this Canada of ours towards a common goal that we can all accept. Let's Do it!!!!!

Can you imagine the result of such a drastic move? People could converse in public places any where in this land in either language without vexing someone because they don't understand. The atmosphere would also improve to the point that each and everyone of us would be proud to declare her or himself a Canadian. Today, in the Province of Quebec, there are people that don't even stand up for the national anthem. This maybe disgraceful to many a Canadian but to those that actually enact this gesture, this is a way of protesting against the Federal Government. You have to be a Quebecer to understand what is going on. Too many individuals outside Quebec have no idea of what it is like to be a resident of the Province and would convert if they had an opportunity to sample the "Love Of Life" syndrome that is the main characteristic of French Canadians. We mustn't forget how Quebec managed through all the years to build up its musical talents and is in the process of doing the same in the film industry. Month after month, French Canadian movie directors are creating films that are getting high ratings not only in Quebec but all over Canada. This is a positive undertaking and can only be a plus for the unity of the country.

Quebec, being the only French faction in Canada, must be assured in the possibility of the project of bilingualism being accepted, must be able to know who the people are and where their roots come from. Only with this assurance will the Province think of going ahead with this proposition. Of course, this important step must also apply to the other Provinces and Territories. The respect for each others origins and beliefs can only enhance the harmony that would install itself among all those involved. We are, actually, all immigrants in Canada and associate ourselves with other continents such as Europe, Asia and so on. Keeping traditions that originate from these far away places is very acceptable because it enables our country men to learn about different ways of living. However; we must not impose these traditions on our fellow citizens due to the fact that we are now Canadians and we must advertise the Canadian way of life that we have adopted. This Canadian way of life happened to be a savior for many people from war torn Europe who settled here and raised families and continued their life lines. A great part of these immigrants came to Canada to work in the mines or became farmers. The proof of this is that a great deal of these people headed to North-Western Quebec and Northern Ontario to work in the gold mines. Out West, a large number of Europeans chose to live off the land. In North-western Quebec, a lot of the off-spring of the immigrants married into French families and have created new generations of bilingual children. These young persons are not affected by the "Separation Question" because they are bilingual and switch from one language to the other at a Moment's notice. Canada is on the verge of a mining boom and this will oblige the Government to expand immigration due to the lack of manpower. If we act fast enough, we could implement this new system rapidly and reap the benefits in the immediate future.

Our country has the potential for major growth and with its land mass it can offer space for an x number of newcomers who could settle down near future developments and make a life for themselves and their families in a country known for treating everyone as equals. This happening would be a win-win situation helping the country to grow prosper for many years to come.

Many employees involved in the forest industry have sought employment in the mining field because the forest industry has petered out and no longer presents a safe outlook in the near future. This stand still has drained the workforce, sadly of course, but eventually will rebound with dire consequences. Those who had lost their jobs in the past will most likely not return for fear of another downturn. Once again, the country will have to offer employment to citizens in other countries to replenish the industry with qualified workers. This is another example if we have the bilingualism project in place, we will be in the position to integrate these immigrants into our society quite easily.

The Separatists in the Province of Quebec are augmenting their drive to win the next election and might even succeed due to the negative popularity of the present Prime Minister. They probably realize that they must get their message across as soon as possible so that they can offer Separation to the Quebec people who seem very disenchanted with the Government of the day. The governing Party, the Liberals at the Moment, have forced unpopular legislation on the students and general public which may cost them dearly at the polls. Time is of the essence and supporters of a united Canada will have to get the wheels turning to convince Quebecers that their language and culture can thrive as well as the other language and culture sharing this great land. The Central Government of Canada is equally facing the loss of interest in

Quebec and the warning to Federalists is quite obvious in the public surveys. The people of Canada have to involve themselves in getting the message out to their respective political representatives that action must be taken to counteract the measures taken by the "Partie Quebecois" who are flirting with the cause of Separation because the timing is ripe. If we let this group succeed, we will all be sorry in the future when we will watch our country fall apart. Deep down inside, nobody wants to see a divided Canada yet the strain of global unrest may just push Quebec to opt out of the federation without actually knowing what the consequences may be.

A Separate Quebec would be a disaster for the country and capital would exit its borders because Quebecers do not know the consequences of such a move. Separatists preach their platform only to show English Canada that they will not be assimilated but not one of their members could foretell the consequences of such a vital decision. Everyone in Canada knows that Quebec identifies itself as being different than the rest of the country.

However; if we were to compare all the regions of Canada we would be surprises how much all of them are not carbon copies. The only thing that is a major obstacle between Quebec and Canada is the language barrier and we know that. The Federal Government, in the last couple of years, declared Quebec a Nation which in itself is true. That was the first step towards keeping Canada as one country. It is now time to take the next step and create bilingualism through out this land and bring it to heights, economically and socially, that nobody would dream of. Then and only then, will we have peace and harmony and last but not least true equality that we as a collectivety believe essential to make everyone feel at home. Otherwise, if Quebec should become a separate state, there will be instability for years and years and could you imagine the court battles related to what belongs to whom. My God, the enormous sums of money spent on the justice system to iron out the substantial problems would be devastating.

The impact of a Separation would go as far as alienating families whose members would disagree with one another. Fathers against sons, brothers against brothers, brothers against sisters etc . . . are only some of the consequences that would grow from such a situation. Quebec would be surrounded by the rest of Canada and would be forced to do business in English which would be another blow to the language barrier. Turning this country into a bilingual one seems to be the easiest of many solutions and would be everlasting. Today people travel much more than in the past and are exposed to different languages across the world. The English and French languages are two dialects heard quite profusely anywhere one travels. How many Quebecers say "I wish I could speak English". A lot of them deprive themselves of travelling to English speaking countries in fear not to be understood. There are more French Canadians then we think that would like to speak English and have their children speak it to. Why doesn't the Separatist Party ask the question in a referendum, simply, they know what the results would be. Maybe many people don't know but politicians are like the Pied Piper, hypnotizing the public and the party that succeeds is the one who did a better job of it. We have, right now, some young politicians who can work this project until we succeed in implementing it. As a matter of fact we have one politician who is fluently bilingual, son of a former Prime Minister and very popular with the public and that of course is Justin Trudeau. The fact that he is a young Quebecer, well educated and has roots elsewhere in the country, make him an ideal candidate to understand what has to be done to rid us of this language sickness. He is a federal member of parliament and in recent polls proved very popular in public polls. Furthermore, the media is reporting that the Liberal party would fair very well in Quebec with him at its helm. We, Canadians, should grasp this excellent occasion to unveil this program and test the will of the electorate to adopt the solution. Justin Trudeau would more than likely adhere to this plan if demanded by the people. If elected as Prime Minister, he could present the program to the country and if it was accepted all the steps needed to get it on its way could be put in place sending Canada on its way to bilingualism.

Mind you, this is not going to be an overnight solution but will prove the best solution from one generation to another. Quebecers will be able to travel anywhere in Canada without needing a translator to communicate and of course it would be easier for Canadians travelling to Quebec. No more bickering, no more tantrums associated with not being understood. Year after year we will notice how the kids between schools will be able to interlock and socialize freely with those from other schools. This definitely can be done and if everyone who loves this country called Canada would participate, they will take the necessary actions for it to happen. The language solution must be the method chosen to solve the dilemma and is truly the simplest action to take to resolve once and for all the differences that have plagued Canadians for as long as we can remember. Pride and joy must replace hate and confrontation between Quebec and the rest of Canada. These qualities will raise our hopes and aspirations thus elevating our hopes and desires by encouraging us to advance to heights never seen in this country. We are all aware that team work has forever outdone individualism and the outcome is much more gainful. When this comes about, then and only then, will we be able to celebrate the birthday of Canada in the true meaning of the word.

In a new Canada, Quebecers will continue to celebrate St. John the Baptist Day to honour their patron saint but the festivities will take on a complete new look as it won't be necessary to use this holiday as a protest against the rest of Canada. Then a week later the whole of Canada, including Quebec, could gather in cities and towns and express their happiness to live in a country that would be the envy of the world.

The language solution would, yes indeed, alter the present way of life of Canadians but the change would be to everyone's advantage. All the money spent in the past on referendums and advertising in both camps could have been allotted to better educate our students and to make life a bit easier for our senior citizens. We must realize that a great number of our seniors are having a hard time making ends meet because they are catalogued as living below the poverty level. In this day and age, it is sinful not to be able to thank our elderly people for having helped to build this nation strong and free.

Economically, investors would flock back to Quebec knowing that the language solution would bring stability in all sectors of activity. This wealth would enable the creation of jobs permitting the country to continue to grow and prosper. Due to the fact that the language problem would be on its way into the history books, the provinces and territories could work hand in hand to develop projects that would augment the revenues of the levels of government thus decreasing our national debt that is unbelievable at the present time. Furthermore, with abundant employment opportunities, we could decrease unemployment and social welfare. People who are motivated tend to want to be part of the solution and not the problem. In the past, we had have not provinces who relied heavily on the Federal Government for their existence. However; these Provinces have now discovered oil in their proximity and no longer need the Federal aid. The most important point, economically, is that we gain from our natural resources and keep the riches here in Canada and not allow foreigners to profit from what is ours. Another result of this choice would keep young people in their regions after obtaining an education because with the economy being strong, these individuals could find work at home.

The artistic world, especially in Quebec, would benefit by increases in the recording field selling more albums in French then ever before. French Canadian singing artists are very good at their trade and excel in all kinds of music. Celine Dion is probably the best example as she has captured the interest of the globe. She started her career in Quebec but as she became more and more popular she recorded in English and has become a Super Star at home and abroad. Many more French Canadians could probably follow the same path having the natural talent that it takes to do so. French stand up comics are some of the world's best. They perform in a way that truly Quebecois in style and quite hilarious at that. Here again would be an opportunity to sell the French Canadian culture which is by all means quite interesting. The language solution would only be a plus for the arts and would allow both cultures to express themselves without any prejudice. The exchange of cultures would most likely help both parties to get to know and understand each other as it should be amongst people living in the same country. One of the Ten Commandments states that we should "Love our neighbour as our self" which makes a lot of common sense when we contemplate its meaning. Friendship has to exist to provide a person with security and the knowledge that he or she is part of the community. We rely on friends when we are in need and offer our help when others are in need creating a human bond that is long lasting and fruitful. Without this characteristic we would be nobodies looking for a meaning in our lives. The associations we involve ourselves in give us the opportunity to be part of the population dwelling in our midst and adding to the successful emancipation of everyone we know. The more friends we have the better is the right attitude to take when we are dealing with our fellowmen, it is pleasant to be able to converse with such persons discussing mutual interests. It also quite often leads to upgrade our cognizance on certain matters and gives us new experiences. Human nature impedes us to have friends to fulfill our social needs and be regarded as an acceptable fun loving neighbour.

In past, many of our Prime Ministers came from French origins and this did not affect the way English Canada voted. If the English faction was stubbornly against French involvement what so ever, it would never allow the election of a French Prime Minister. Therefore, this is proof that English Canada holds no grudge against the French and would probably adhere to the language solution without hesitation. Politicians is do not dwell on this topic because they fear the consequents of their decisions not knowing if they will please the electorate. The politician who will submit the language solution to his party's platform will definitely find a place in the history books. Yet, it is a simple step to take if one truly believes that this is the way to go about unifying the country and solving the linguistic context that is eating up little the patience of the Canadian people. We have nothing to lose by testing this answer to have common sense prevail. It would be a start in the right direction and could and would be acceptable by everyone concerned. Let's face it, nothing has been done to alleviate this burden we carry day in and day out, hoping that it will go away but before you know it, it pops up right back and then we know that it is still there without anything being done to make it go away. We have to force the hands of our representatives both in Ottawa and the provinces to consult the electorate as to what should be done to remedy the impasse. The Canadian people should demand a referendum to verify if the whole country is willing to give the program a chance to succeed. Following a referendum and depending on its result the appropriate measures to deal with it should be adopted. If the majority opt for the solution, the proper authorities would negotiate how they would go about to implement it and in a time lapse that is reasonable. A committee could be chosen with all the parties naming a negotiator to represent them. Once the plan of action put in place, the results would have to become law and we would be on our way to creating a bilingual Canada.

However; if the referendum failed to pick up the necessary votes, depending on who made it fail, we would as a collectivity have to face the music and live with the consequences of our decision. Frankly, though, the odds would be in favour of accepting rather than refusing because the numbers show that people are open minded when it comes to learning a new language. If there is a free choice, we can almost bet that a great part of the population will be most willing to have their children graduating from high School with the ability to speak, read and write in both founding tongues. Once again it must be pointed out that by achieving this goal, Canada could save billions of dollars and reduce the national debt substantially.

In another context, if Quebec's majority or the rest of Canada's voted against installing such a project, Quebec's separation would be imminent but not without any costs. Investors would move their money to another province and there is no telling if there would be pain or gain. The exit of capital would be humongous and nobody knows how this would affect Quebec's economy. The Quebec population should demand that the Separatists prove to them what effect the outcome of this action would be. If the Quebec economy crumbles and the unemployment rate surges to new heights, how does the Partie Quebecois remedy this. The separation issue has never been explained thoroughly as to the impact it will have on the province because the fanatics that are trying to make it happen are themselves unaware of the end result. They are trying, by acting as nationalists to persuade the masses to follow them blindly into the unknown. They use the language difference to display the fact that Quebec and Canada can not succeed to live side by side because they will be assimilated. Nothing is more a falsehood than such a thought, you can not alter a person's belief just because you outnumber her or him. Language is a means of communication and if used on a daily basis can not be forgotten by the flick of a wand. Quebec definitely has a place in Canada and need not worry of being assimilated but needs to be assured of its right to use the French language in the province. Losing one's culture as a direct result of being a minority is a ridiculous myth and does not stand as a reason to break up a country. But, losing one's language rights is seriously a concern and must be death with by law which would be unanimously accepted by adopting the Language Solution. The French in Quebec must open their eyes and observe what the Partie Quebecois is really about and not give the power to opt out of Canada primarily due to sentiments. If they do so, they will be jeopardizing their future and the generations to follow. The Language Solution would have two winners as compared to Separation which would be a lose-lose proposition, The Partie Quebecois should be required to inform the citizens of Quebec what measures it intends to use to comport its option of exiting Confederation. It also must have legal proof that this move will not ruin what the people of the province worked so hard to accomplish. If we base ourselves on what exists today, the Partie Quebecois does not have any kind of documentation that unveils the after Separation era. It is trying to sell its idea strictly by playing on the sentiments of the province's people. This tactic could come back and haunt it if the Province was to separate and be affected negatively. We mustn't forget the credo of our politicians "Do what I say and not what I do". There are members of the Partie Quebecois that sent their children to schools outside of Quebec. Are they trying to imitate the Church back in the forties and fifties who controlled the population by brainwashing. Today, young people are very well educated so this path would be scrutinized very thoroughly before being accepted.

There are several English speaking Quebecers that marry French girls because the latter are less conservative than English speaking women. This is rather true for males of European descent who were raised in the Province of Quebec. These marriages, in general, turn out offspring that becomes bilingual at a very young age. Then the next generation is also bilingual, hence, the Language Solution. The answer is there, it is obvious and simple, children at a young age can learn many dialects making them the envy of those who only speak one. For Canada to grow and prosper more then ever, the whole country has to come to a consensus that there must be changes in the way we communicate. We have to emphasize that both English and French are the working tongues and make this the law of the land for future generations. Then and only then, will we have created the true identity of being a Canadian in the real sense of the word. A new bilingual Canadian society would been born and we could muster our energies towards improving our economy and making it one of the richest in the world.

In the last couple of years, most of the people immigrating to Canada are of Asian descent. The numbers are so huge that they are asking to continue all their tradition, cultural and religious, to be recognised and respected by us. This makes no sense but our country allowed them certain rights and now it is being blown out of proportion. The immigrants from Europe came here, adapted to Canada's ways and promoted their cultures by building halls and practising their traditions there. Their kids went to English or French schools, attended church at their congregations and followed traditions at home. Enough is enough, if these new immigrants want to impose their way of life on us, we should say sorry but we can not accept that. People who wish to immigrate to Canada must do so with the intention to adapt to the Canadian style of living or be refused entry. If we start to grant special permissions to different ethnics, we will end up altering what we want our Canada to be like. We respect the Charter of Rights and do not prevent these newcomers to practise their beliefs, however; we deplore the idea of having to accept them as these immigrants would like. Canadians are not racist nor prejudice but still, they are aware that if they chose to live in Asia they would be asked to comply with the way of living over there. Yes, we welcome Asian immigrants to Canada but insist that they have to adhere to our laws and principles. This way we would all be proud to be "Canadian citizens" who are respected alike, governed by the same laws and especially equal to each other which would form a bond amongst population of the country.

CONCLUSION

The time has arrived to end the threat of Separation and get on with the business of living in a country that is our homeland wide and free and where people want to be because of its freedom and equality. We should commence lobbying our Government officials starting now and pressuring them to introduce the Language Solution as a bill in the near future. The sooner we make this happen, the faster will our children reap the benefits of such an audacious project that will change the face of Canada forever. We must not let up if we intend to keep Canada strong economically and free in language in order to attract immigrants with great knowledge to help us expand the wealth that is omnipresent. Every sector of our day to day economy will show dramatic increase in activity and, if we play it right, decrease unemployment to a trickle. This in turn will create wealth thus enabling all the citizens of Canada to benefit equally. The country could alleviate poverty of many seniors who simply can not make ends meet in their present predicament. These individuals spent a life time improving our standard of living and are entitled to a fair share of the country's wealth with the great variety of natural resources, minerals, oil, natural gas and so on, available for the taking, we can offer these people a better subsistence than they have now. The time is ripe to take this step because the Canadian population is comprised of a large number of elderly people and this will increase as the "Baby Boomers" fall into retirement.

The Language Solution is not a bandage to help heal the differences between our founding ancestors but a concrete leap into solving all those years of bickering in the political field which has resulted in distaste of the Central Government and Quebec. If we let this continue, the population in Quebec will, this is almost positive, give the Partie Quebecois the opportunity to give Separation a go. Once that becomes reality, the remaining parts of Canada will slowly pull away from Confederation and we do not know at what cost. Is that what we want? No, absolutely not, so let's give this program a try and we will come out of this winners for ourselves and the generations that will follow. Canadians will be prouder then ever and strangers will stop questioning us about the subject of breaking up. The part of the Canadian anthem "Our home and native land" will apply, as it should, to everyone who chooses to be a part of it.

Lately, there has been a boom in developing the far North and the Quebec Liberals have devised a project called Plan Nord in which the Government would participate to help mining companies that are making discoveries to start up. This is truly a well thought out investment that will fill up Government coffers in the coming future. We do not want to see the question of Separation scare away potential participants in this development. The far North development will require another increase in the workforce like we have never seen before. Right now, mines like Raglan (Xtrata), Meadow Banks (Agnico Eagle) and others are having difficulties recruiting candidates to fill vacant positions. Therefore, they will have to look outside the country to find qualified personnel. The total population in Canada will rise substantially and the increase will enclose workers from all over this planet. Now, more than ever, is the occasion to subscribe to the installation of a Language Solution which will be acceptable for those concerned. If we want people to come and live their lives in Canada, we must definitely demonstrate that we are united and trying to attain the same goals. Otherwise, these persons will be reluctant to relocate to a country that is fighting internally and is in turmoil. The answer is right there for the taking, at the tip of our hands. Yes, The Language Solution is by far the route to take to interest capable candidates to become a part of a workforce that will grow in numbers and consist of immigrants from the four corners of the globe. They will earn the right to learn both English and French unless they already use one of these dialects in which case they would apprehend the other. They would be traded as equals and after the required time lapse would be sworn in as full fledged Canadians.

In this whole matter, there is but one hic, Quebecers, in the majority of cases, do not believe in the Status Quoi for the Monarchy and that is their prerogative. They should not be forced to recognize Elizabeth as their Queen. There are enormous amounts of money spent on regal visits to Canada and a vast majority of Canadians probably feel that these sums could be used for precise domestic purposes. It is enough that Quebec has a Governor General who represents the Queen something that should be abolished. As a matter of fact, the last Governor General has been accused of misusing public funds and is bring dragged through court for that reason.

The Language Solution should not frighten anyone, it is a simple undertaking of educating our children which is probably acceptable to the great majority of Canadians. Furthermore, people who immigrate to this wonderful Canada of ours would also have to take up the two dialogues, if needed. There it is in a nutshell, The Language Solution or ?????????

EPILOGUE

The author still resides in the Province of Quebec, has many friends that are Anglophone, Francophone and bilingual. It is funny because those who are unilingual keep saying that they wish they could speak both languages. The French in Quebec can not send their kids to English school and the teaching of the English tongue in the French classroom sucks. The rest of Canada offers an education in the French language only where it is warranted. The teaching of the French language in English schools also sucks. The citizens of Quebec who are educated in English are given the right to send their children to English schools and this permission is passed on to the following generations.

The author learned his French in High School because he had a professor (Fernand Bourgeault) who was devoted to his job of making Frenchmen out of his English students. He was a very interesting person who always managed to keep the attention of his class. So to render to Caesar what belongs to Caesar, this is why this writer would like to dedicate this work to the late Mr. Bourgeault who is very much responsible for this author being fluently bilingual.

His unselfishness and candour moulded many an English student into using the French dialect with unbelievable ease. One year, there was a girl from Toronto, who only spoke English of course, started school in

September and was not allowed to speak English which was a mortal sin in Mr. Bourgeault's class, and yes, before you knew it, she was able to converse in French. Lord what a great man!!!!!!!

The author also was inspired by John Lennon's song "Imagine" that mentions himself as a dreamer but not the only one. Hell yes, he maybe is a dreamer yet there surely are more dreamers in this Canada of opportunities who see the vision of a bilingual country in the next generation.

God bless Fernand Bourgeault, John Lennon and the whole of Canada. We were put on this earth as equals and the religion beliefs state that we are brothers and sisters so let us act accordingly. Let's not allow our politicians use the Language problem to throw us against each other. We will be the big winners if we accept each other for what we are and work together to solve out differences.

www.ingramcontent.com/pod-product-compliance
Lightning Source LLC
LaVergne TN
LVHW092101060526
838201LV00047B/1505